Colourful AUSTRIA

INTRODUCTION AND EXPLANATORY NOTES BY

HERBERT BUZAS

HISTORICAL NOTES BY

DR. MARIA NEUSSER-HROMATKA

PINGUIN-VERLAG, INNSBRUCK/TYROL

TRANSLATED FROM THE GERMAN BY RICHARD RICKETT

FOR THE ARRANGEMENT AND CHECKING OF THE SELECTION "AUSTRIA DOWN THE CENTURIES"
THANKS ARE DUE TO:

DR. O. MENGHIN
PROFESSOR DR. K. PIVEC
DR. MARIA DAWID

SELECTION OF PICTURES AND CAPTIONS BY MILA LIPPMANN-PAWLOWSKI AND HERBERT BUZAS

PEN- AND INK DRAWINGS BY RAGONIG

FRONT COVER: THE RUINED CASTLE OF AGGSTEIN ON THE DANUBE
PHOTOGRAPH BY ROBERT LÖBL

BACK COVER: A PASTURE AT THE FOOT OF THE WILDER KAISER, TYROL
PHOTOGRAPH BY TONI SCHNEIDERS

THE PICTURE ON THE FRONTISPIECE SHOWS THE VORDERE GOSAUSEE
AND THE DACHSTEIN MASSIF
PHOTOGRAPH: HEINZ MÜLLER-BRUNKE

PRINTED AND MADE IN AUSTRIA BY THE
WAGNER'SCHE UNIV.-BUCHDRUCKEREI BUCHROITHNER & CO., INNSBRUCK

SOME OF THE STEREOTYPE-PLATES WERE PREPARED BY THE FIRM OF R. SEYSS, VIENNA

SAMUM ART PAPER "POLYTON"

THE WORLD OF THE AUSTRIAN

Austria is a small country. Showing it in a pocket-sized Atlas is a cartographer's nightmare; and driving across it at its narrowest point takes the motorist little longer than he needs to do justice to a substantial packed lunch. The tourist who joins the East-bound express on the shores of Lake Constance will easily be in Vienna by sundown. That's how small Austria is.

Austria, a name not infrequently confused with Australia in the world at large, is the home of some 7 million people, an insignificant fraction of the world's total population of 2½ milliards. Yet to be born one of those 7 million can be accounted a stroke of luck, especially if in the course of one's life one attains the status of a "professional" Austrian. It means making few enemies in the world, and so being able to devote one's energies to coping with one's friends, which is an extremely comforting thought.

Peace and Quiet, those twin gifts of the gods which nowadays the hustler nips in the bud at the dawn of each hectic day, still reign in Austria: but they are not something you can buy, hygienically packed, in a chemist's shop; they are part and parcel of a hereditary way of life that characterises and distinguishes the professional Austrian, a man to whom anything that smacks of disturbance or upheaval—such as philosophers with high-flown ideas about making the world a better place—is equally abhorrent. From the first he regards all such ideas with the greatest suspicion and loses no time in adapting them to his own requirements, in smoothing over the rough edges, damping down over-exuberance, and setting reasonable limits to extravagance. Which is why dangerous "isms" cut less ice in Austria than elsewhere; why even radicals never tear up the tree roots and all; why pestilences that corrupt the mind, and threats of force, are for the most part innocuous; why the skyscrapers in Austria are stunted, the caprices of fashion less outrageous, and the social contrasts less glaring than in some other countries. And the Austrian knows how to make even dictatorship tolerable and humane.

The professional Austrian is a past-master in the art of adjustment; and the adjustment of contradictions makes for tolerance. He tolerates the next-door neighbour without making a fuss about it, and leaves him to his quaint beliefs, his delusions, his prejudices, and his errors. In Austria tolerance is as precious as a good drop of wine: in fact, in the country you can even find inn-signs with the unusual inscription "Zur Toleranz." And it would need the patience and persistence of a Diogenes to find among the 7 million citizens of this small country anyone ostentatious enough to flaunt his political convictions in the form of a badge. The Austrian prefers to decorate his hat with a chamois-brush, with a souvenir of the last shoot or of the last Kandahar ski-race. Yet he is well aware that in theory the first person he runs across in the street is almost certain to cherish political beliefs diametrically opposed to his own, for the two parties that determine the Austrian political climate are almost equal in strength, which means that everything has to be nicely balanced: equilibrium on the fence must be preserved at all costs. Normally, this too makes for peace and quiet; but what happens when for once a definite decision has to be made, yes or no? The professional Austrian is an adept at extricating himself from such an uncouth situation, and if the worst comes to the worst and he has to choose one of two alternatives, he will choose—the third. Another victory for compromise, another triumph of adjustment. But this is an Austrian patent, and not very suitable for export.

Geographically, Austria is a space between two Festivals. From the floating-stage at Bregenz there is a view of the Swiss and Bavarian shores of Lake Constance, while the lake-side stage at Mörbisch on the Neusiedler See in Burgenland breathes the air of the Great Hungarian Plain. Austria's Festival equator also passes through the Domplatz at Salzburg and touches Vienna, the Mecca of the musical world. It could almost be called a line of latitude on the map of European festivals. Now Festivals in Austria are not just summer finery, something to be taken out of the wardrobe at certain seasons of the year and cleaned and brushed up for the occasion. They spring from the Austrian addiction to things artistic, from the possession of a precious heritage in which great works of art are preserved and venerated. From one end of the country to the other there is hardly a village without some objet d'art, hardly a town without something to delight the eye. Every one of the provinces contains cultural monuments well worth a visit. But Vienna, the Imperial city of old and to-day, in American eyes, the most "European" city on the continent, is worth more than just a visit. To a man of culture, Vienna presents a field of research that will last him a lifetime. In Vienna, the Austrian can feel proud of being a citizen of a cultural Great Power.

But all this is a shade too highbrow. The Austrian, amid the sunny, smiling landscape of his native land, has a predilection for light, graceful, lilting rhythms of the kind for instance that give Viennese music its characteristic flavour, so that when the world waltzes, it is round Austria that it revolves. The melodies of Johann Strauss, Lehár, and others, are musical exports that find a ready market the world over. Good form, musical as well as social, "made in Austria," is a speciality of this small country.

Here in this "land of dancers, land of fiddlers," the love of graceful, elegant design extends to the smallest objects of everyday use. The small silver coins, for instance, are stamped with the smiling features of the "Wachau Queen" (a girl wearing the golden head-dress of Lower Austrian national costume), or with a horseman of the historic Spanish Riding-school, with his white stallion rearing in a levade that is as light as a passing thought. Small, often unnoticed works of art, that pass from hand to hand. And from ear to ear passes the interval signal of the Austrian radio, an air from one of Mozart's operas. The genius of Grillparzer is remembered in the old Austrian military manual, while the tune played by the cornet in the band of the Austrian army of to-day comes from Haydn. In Austria the Muses, like the Saints, are regarded as part of the family, venerated with the same devotion in the Burgtheater as on the smallest provincial stage; in the Vienna Opera and concert halls as in the rehearsal-room of an obscure country choir in Carinthia; in Cathedrals, monasteries, and chapels as in the crucifix corner of a peasant parlour. They are cultivated by high society and by the middle classes as assiduously as by the great company of unpretentious citizens lower down in the social scale.

And technology? Where does technology come in, in a country where the best instrument for a real understanding of the inhabitants is the violin? The Austrian never mentions technology unless he is asked about it. He finds it distasteful to boast of achievements which, by their very unexpectedness, will cause surprise and embarrassment. Austria's contribution, in regions reminiscent of the Ice Age, to the welfare of humanity are passed over in silence; little is said of the gigantic schemes by which water from melting glaciers is stored up in reservoirs and converted into power for export. Whenever visiting VIP's begin to open their eyes and their mouths in astonishment at one of the gigantic hydraulic power-stations, the Austrian allows himself a complacent but furtive smirk. How is the world at large to know that in tiny Austria riveres both sluggish and turbulent are made to work in their courses? How many people know about the Austrian equivalent of Kuwait, with its forest of steel towers among the vineyards, and oceans of oil waiting to be tapped? Austrian engineers have been responsible for some of the speediest and most daring cable-railways in the whole of the Alps (with apologies for the superlatives); while the Grossglockner road is one of the wonders of Europe. No: technology has not come striding into the country in seven-league boots; its approach has been diffident, and as noiseless as that of those prehensile rubber soles that enable mountaineers to penetrate slowly but surely the remotest mountain solitude.

The visitor from abroad takes it for granted that a special sort of friendly good-humour is permanent and indigenous in Austria. Nor will he be disappointed; only he must realise that each of the various peoples inhabiting the part of Europe between the rivers March and Rhine has its own special brand of good-humour: the pensive taciturnity of the dwellers in remote mountain valleys, the tears of the gypsy fiddler, the exultant shout of the yodler, the sentimental "stick together through thick and thin" type of song, and the fraternal affinity of hearts that beat in unison. It can communicate itself in intimate as well as in uproarious company, it may wear leather shorts or a tail-coat, it may be lit by cosy lantern-light or by the kaleidoscopic neon-lights of the big city, it may bubble from a glass of wine or even of mineral water. But wherever it is sensed, its essence is the same: it comes directly from the heart and can only unfold where people have time; haste and hustle are fatal to it. Over Austria the tyranny of the passing second has no sway. Not to let your leisure be interfered with, to take your time and do things at your own convenience, that is the main thing; for "God gave mankind time, but there was nothing said about hurry." The way the Austrian has developed the management of time, this gift from the gods, into a fine art shows that he is verily by the Grace of God a connoisseur in the art of living. Far from killing it, he savours it like a beaker of fine Wachau wine. It is therefore true that good-humour in all its phases can indeed be regarded as a permanent feature of Austria, for what is more permanent than time? Perhaps it is the forest, with its unhurried growth, that has taught the Austrian the value and the essence of time. The forest produces fragrant, homely wood, and the annual circles in the wood and its barely audible creaking are a hint to the convivial company in the parlour, to the lovers on a park-bench, and to the tycoon in the Board-Room, to take it easy, never on any account to be in too much of a hurry. It is no mere coincidence that it is in countries where the forests are protected and wood is precious that good-humour is a feature of even the humblest cottage. And one final observation while on the subject of this subtle quality that foreigners find it difficult even to translate: another reason why visitors find Austria such a good-humoured country is that everything that is not expressly forbidden is allowed. One's thoughts turn to certain other countries where everything is forbidden unless it is expressly allowed.

For nearly fifty years now the Austrians have been living within the constricted frontiers of a Republic that is all that is left of a great Empire. People born after 1910—the majority in fact—can have little or no recollection of Habsburg days. But the traces of the Imperial family that for 600 years helped in Austria to shape the history of the western world are plain for all to see. There is a wealth of Imperial relics to prevent the Austrian from ever losing touch with the past. He remembers the centuries of Habsburg rule for a very characteristic and very human reason: the days of pageantry are easier to remember than the days of suffering. And this is why the Austrian, rather than break abruptly with the past, gently and gradually puts it behind him, rather like a ferryman making cautiously for the further shore: and we Austrians who are his passengers are also setting course for the future. On our journey we take with us a great past and a wealth of experience, chequered with hopes and disappointments.

If we are asked to try to explain what it is that, shorn of all the accretions and accidents of temporary influences, we really feel in our heart of hearts, the answer will be something like this: Austria has no wish to play an important part in world affairs, yet despite a past so full of suffering and misery the Austrian is still fundamentally an incurable optimist, and therefore he thinks that he can best be of service to the world by making his lovely country a place where people from all over the world enjoy meeting each other. As long as people can associate freely, there is peace. The peace-loving Austrian, with his innate cordiality and mental agility, has the knack of reconciling the unreconciled, of bringing together the hitherto incompatible. To-day, when European unity is so much in the air, he would like to find new scope for the skill as a mediator that for centuries he was constrained to exercise in dealings with his fellow-subjects—Roumanians, Slavs, Magyars, etc.—in the Dual Monarchy, and so to help bridge the gulf of misunderstanding between East and West.

Herbert Buzas

5

AUSTRIA DOWN THE CENTURIES

History   Culture

**Late
Stone Age**

Circa 40,000—circa 5000/4000 B.C.

Among a number of excavations of various kinds at
Willendorf, in the Wachau, Lower Austria, were two
female figures, one of which, the so-called "Venus of
Willendorf" of oolithic limestone, has become world-
famous: it is the most naturalistic of all the "Veneres"
so far unearthed.

The Venus of Willendorf

**Late
Stone Age
(neolithic)**

Circa 5000/4000—1800 B.C.

Evidence of numerous peasant settlements in Burgenland,
Lower and Upper Austria, in the Drau valley and in the
Klagenfurt area.

**Early
Bronze Age**

Circa 1800—1300 B.C.

Historical and cultural development is determined by
two main groups: the "Aunjetitz" civilisation abutting
on to the northern part of Lower Austria, but not spreading southwards over the Danube except in its western
area; and the "Straubing" civilisation in Vorarlberg,
North Tyrol, Salzburg and Upper Austria.

The important feature of the "Straubing" civilisation was. its exploitation of Alpine copper resources (ancient mine at Schwaz in Tyrol).

Late
Bronze Age

Circa 1300—750 B.C.

The urn-burial-grounds, found in Austria as well as in most other parts of Europe, have some historical connection (details of which are still unconfirmed) with the great Mass Migrations, and the migrations of the maritime peoples of the Eastern and Central Mediterranean.

Of particular significance are the early urn-fields of North Tyrol near Innsbruck (Wilten, Mühlau, Hötting, Sonnenburg-Natters, Völs, Volders) and the later excavations at Stillfried, Lower Austria, and Maria Rast (Lower Styria). The so-called "Kultwagen von Strettweg" discovered in a tumulus near Judenburg, Styria, belongs to the transition period leading to the Hallstatt civilisation proper.

The Hallstatt
Civilisation
(Early
Iron Age)

Circa 750—400 B.C.

Following the "urn-fields" came a group of civilisations named after the burial-ground near the town of Hallstatt in Upper Austria. From the interplay of various cultural streams, south-German and Venetian in particular, spreading in opposite directions there developed a definite "Hallstatt" civilisation almost identical in area with that of the later Province of Tyrol.

Bronze Kettle. From Hallstatt

The wealth of Hallstatt was derived from salt-trading, and excavations reveal connections with various other groups. Further excavations at Dürrnberg near Hallein also confirm the important part played by salt-mining even in those early days. The Hallstatt tumuli of the "Wieser Gruppe" in Styria are obviously the burial-ground of a noble family.

The
La Tène
period

*Youth from the
Helenenberg*

Circa 400—15 B. C.

During the 5th century B. C. the salt-mines at Dürrnberg must have been taken over by Celts of the early La Tène civilisation, who after peopling the Salzburg area thrust down the Danube at or shortly after the turn of the century. A century later they were spreading southwards through the Alps and founded the kingdom of Noricum with its centre in Carinthia. In Tyrol the indigenous Hallstatt civilisation continued after assimilating elements of the La Tène civilisation. In 102 B. C. the Cimbri and Teutones passed through the land.

The Romans   ↓

15 B. C.—400 A. D.

In 15 B. C. the "Drusus campaign" led to the formation of the Roman province of Rhaetia, to which North Tyrol and Vorarlberg belonged. About the same time as the birth of Christ the kingdom of Noricum was peacefully penetrated and became a Roman province. Establishment of the first Danube frontier from Carnuntum to Boiodorum (Passau) as the northern limit of Roman expansion. Settling of the Province of Pannonia, extending from the eastern frontier of Noricum as far as the Hungarian north-south course of the Danube.

The Celtic town on the Helenenberg near Klagenfurt lasted till about the middle of the 1st century A. D. The highly impressive ruins of Carnuntum include two amphitheatres, a military camp, and a residential quarter (about 10,000 inhabitants probably).

166—180

War against the Marcomanni, who with the Quadi had overrun the Danube frontier. In 180 death of the Emperor and great military commander Marcus Aurelius (? in Vienna).

About 260 the Alemanni, who were constantly pouring over the Roman frontier on the Rhine, set foot for the first time on Austrian soil.

In 313 Christianity, which had been establishing itself in various localities ever since the start of the third century A. D., was declared by the Emperor Constantine to be the State religion. During the fourth century the dioceses of Aguntum near Lienz, Teurnia near Spittal on the Drau, and Virunum on the Zollfeld near Klagenfurt were established.

From about 400 the Austrian territories gradually withdrew from the Roman Empire.

434—453 The Huns under Attila occupy Pannonia and thrust further west, but on the death of Attila his Empire disintegrates.

By 500 the Bajuvars from the west were slowly beginning to infiltrate into the Danube area. After the withdrawal southwards of the Lombards in 568 came an invasion of the Avars from the east, followed by Slav tribes. Tyrol, which since the end of the Ostrogoth Empire in 553 had been loosely associated with Italy, is now placed under the administration of a "Dux Raetiae".

Towards the end of the sixth century the Bajuvars begin to take up defensive positions against the Slavs advancing up the Drau valley and along the Pustertal.

About 700 St. Rupert founds the Benedictine abbey of St. Peter on the ruins of Juvavum and is presented with the remains of the city by Archduke Theodore II of Bavaria.

696—805 The Bavarian bishopric at Salzburg and the Agilolfing Archdukes of Bavaria set about Christianising the pagan Slav and Germanic tribes.

788 Bavaria and Carantania (Carinthia) are incorporated in the Empire of the Franks after the subjugation of Duke Tassilo III.

791—799 Charlemagne conquers the Avars and forms the "Ostmark" bounded by the rivers Enns, Raab, and Drau.

798—811	Salzburg, the intellectual centre of the Franco-Bavarian ecclesiastical province, is constituted an archbishopric under Bishop Arno.
881	Battle between the Franks and the Magyars at "Wenia". Annihilation of the Bavarian levies and disintegration of Charlemagne's "Ostmark" (907).
After 955	Defeat of the Magyars at Lechfeld and reconstitution of the "Ostmark" as a bulwark against them.
976	Elevation of Carinthia to the status of an independent Duchy under the House of Eppensteiner (1077).
1156	Austria is separated from Bavaria by Friedrich Barbarossa and created a hereditary duchy under the Babenberg Margrave Heinrich Jasomirgott.

1000—1093

Among the most important monasteries established by the Babenbergs are Melk (circa 1000), Göttweig (1074), Klosterneuburg (1114), Heiligenkreuz (1135), Admont (1074), Millstatt (1070), St. Paul im Lavanttal (1091), Wilten (1138), and Mehrerau (1093).

1077—1181

Construction of the castles Hohensalzburg, Hohenwerfen, and Petersberg near Friesach.

1130—
circa 1230

Erection of many Romanesque buildings in Salzburg and neighbouring territories. Reconstruction of Salzburg Cathedral after the fire of 1167. Re-building of the Abbey Church of St. Peter at Salzburg (1130—1140). Building of the Cathedral of Gurk in Carinthia with three naves and a crypt containing 100 pillars (1140—1200): of the Church and cloisters of Millstatt Monastery (1120—1170): of the basilicas of the Benedictine Abbeys at Seckau, Styria (1150—1164), and St. Paul im Lavanttal, Carinthia (1180—1230).

The crypt of Gurk Cathedral

Circa 1160—1200	The artistically-minded Babenbergs make their capital at Vienna, an important centre of Danube trade with the Orient, and situated on the route to the Holy Land taken by the first crusading armies. The Nibelung saga is woven into epic form, probably at Passau.
1220—1260	Late flowering of south-German Romanesque in the Danube lands: the west-front of St. Stephen's Cathedral in Vienna, with a wealth of figurative decoration above the doorway: the Great Door (1230—1260): the Romanesque naves of the Michaelerkirche in Vienna and of the Liebfrauenkirche at Wiener Neustadt (circa 1250).
1220— circa 1300	First appearance of Gothic in Austria. For the Vienna Court of Leopold VI an architect from Burgundy designs the cloisters of Lilienfeld and Heiligenkreuz, the Babenberger ducal palace (almost entirely destroyed) at Klosterneuburg, and the "Capella speziosa", also at Klosterneuburg.
1246	Frederick the Quarrelsome, the last Babenberg, is killed fighting the Magyars under Bela IV on the battlefield of the Leitha.

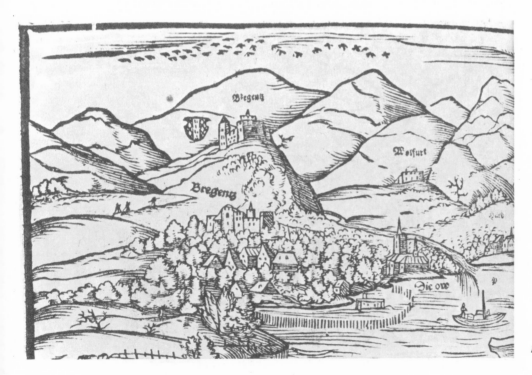

Bregenz

1276—1282   Following his victory over King Ottocar of Bohemia on the Marchfeld in 1276, King Rudolf of Habsburg occupies the Babenberg lands and confers Austria and Styria on his son Albrecht, the beginning of the rule of the House of Habsburg.

1300—1340   The Albertine Choir of St. Stephen's Cathedral (1304—1340) and the Augustinerkirche (1340) in Vienna.

1300—   The golden age of High Gothic sculpture and painting:
circa 1340   the "Servants' Madonna" in St. Stephen's Cathedral, the Virgin at Klosterneuburg, the shrine of St. Florian in the Monastery of St. Florian, the Virgin and Child from the Monastery of Admont (in the Joanneum at Graz), and the Nonnberg crucifix at Salzburg.

1349   The Great Plague

1342   Margrave Ludwig of Brandenburg, husband of Margarethe Maultasch, issues the oldest known ordinance in Tyrol, the so-called "Grand Proclamation of Freedom," assuring equal political rights for all communities and individuals.

1358—1365   Rudolf "the Founder" purports to have proof of Austrian sovereignty and claims the title of Archduke of Austria. Acquisition of Tyrol from Margarethe Maultasch (1365).

Linz

1359— circa 1440	The golden age of the Habsburg capital of Vienna under Rudolf IV and the rulers in the Albertinian line.
1359—1467	Completion of the main aisle of St. Stephen's Cathedral, Vienna, which finally takes shape as a spacious edifice with three naves, three choirs, richly-ornamented pediments (1430) and a lofty, tapering south tower, the greatest example of German Late-Gothic in south-east Europe. The foundation-stone of the nave extension laid by Archduke Rudolf IV (1359).
1379	The partition of Austria between Rudolf's brothers Albrecht III and Leopold III, the former receiving Upper and Lower Austria, and the latter Tyrol, Styria, Carinthia, Krain, and the ancestral Habsburg domains on the Upper Rhine.
1380—1390	The Counts of Bregenz dispose of their rights in the Bregenzerwald and of their property at Feldkirch to the House of Habsburg (Leopold III).
1477	Acquisition of the Netherlands and the Franche-Comté of Burgundy through the marriage of the Archduke Maximilian, the son of the Emperor Friedrich III, to Maria, the only daughter of Charles the Bold.

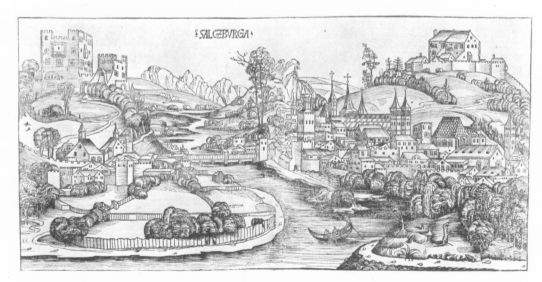

Salzburg

1480—1490   King Matthias Corvinus of Hungary occupies Lower
Austria and Styria and attempts to rule his empire from
Vienna during the years of famine 1480—1490.

The Emperor Friedrich III flees to Graz (the Burg dates
from 1483), and from 1490 makes Wiener Neustadt,
"the ever faithful," his capital, where the young King
Maximilian is later received as liberator.

1479—1519   The great days of Tyrol, under Duke Sigmund "the rich
in coin" and his relative and successor Maximilian
(1490—1519). Innsbruck, the Emperor's favourite residence, is the seat of the "Upper Austrian" administration.
Gun-foundry and Court armoury at Mühlau (from 1490).

1481—1515   The last days of Gothic and the dawn of a new era.

Triptych altar at St. Wolfgang by Michael Pacher. The
Kefermarkt (Upper Austria) altar (1490—circa 1500).
The marble tomb of the Emperor Friedrich III in St. Ste-
phen's Cathedral, Vienna, as well as the base of the organ
(1513) and pulpit (circa 1515) by the Cathedral architect
Anton Pilgram.

Innsbruck

1497—1500   Foundation of the Imperial "Hofkapelle" in Vienna by
Maximilian I.

1499—1515   The Habsburgs acquire an Empire by a series of shrewd
marriages. Through Philip of Habsburg's marriage to
Juana of Castile the Habsburgs acquire the Spanish

Empire with its possessions in America and Naples (1499). Through the double marriage between Maximilian's grandchildren Ferdinand and Maria and the children of the Jagellon King, Ludwig and Anna, Bohemia and Hungary in due course pass to Austria.

Maximilian I

1500—1516   Acquisition from Bavaria of the mining districts of Kufstein and Kitzbühel; and of Lienz and the Gorizian territories on the Isonzo by the Emperor Maximilian. Organisation of the defence of Tyrol (conscription and local militia) by the "Landlibell" of 1511.

1508—1550   The Emperor Maximilian, as a "permanent memorial" to posterity, has his tomb, since become world-famous, prepared in the Hofkirche at Innsbruck.

1522   The House of Habsburg separates into two distinct lines, Ferdinand receiving the Arch-Duchy of Austria above and below the river Enns, Styria, Carinthia, and Krain.

1526   The inherited territories of Bohemia, Silesia, and Hungary pass legally into the possession of Austria on the death of the last Jagellon King Ludwig II. Birth of the Danube Monarchy.

Vienna

	History	Culture
1529	Sultan Suleiman besieges Vienna, but is repulsed by Graf Niklas Salm-Reifferscheid.	
1533	Vienna restored to its position as capital by Ferdinand I after a break of 100 years.	
1541		Death in Salzburg of the famous doctor Theophrastus, the founder of medical chemistry.
1558—1566		Foundation of the Court Library and the Habsburg art collection.
1570—1580	The Emperor Maximilian allows the aristocracy in Upper and Lower Austria freedom of religion.	
1571	The people of Vienna appeal for religious toleration.	

Graz

Klagenfurt

1587—1612

Mediaeval Salzburg is transformed by Archbishop Wolf Dietrich into an Italianate Court residence. Widening of the Cathedral Square (1600) and enlargement of the archiepiscopal Residence (completed under Marcus Sitticus in 1619). Building of the Mirabell Palace and the memorial chaped to Wolf Dietrich in the cemetery of St. Sebastian.

1614—1628

Reconstruction of the Cathedral at Salzburg on the foundations of the former Romanesque basilica by Santino Solari in early Italian Baroque style. Solari also builds the country palace of Hellbrunn with its famous fountains (circa 1615).

1640—1664

Lodovico Burnacini builds the first Imperial Opera House, seating 5,000 spectators.

Prince Eugene

17

1679	According to contemporary, and probably exaggerated estimates, the Plague from Hungary claimed 100,000 victims in Vienna.
1683	Vienna is again besieged by the Turks, this time commanded by the Grand Vizier Kara Mustapha. After a heroic defence by Graf Ernst Rüdiger von Starhemberg the city is relieved by an army coming down from the Kahlenberg, consisting of the Imperial forces and their Polish, Saxon, Bavarian, Swabian, and Frankish allies.
1697—1718	After Prince Eugene's glorious victories over the Turks at Zenta (1697), Peterwardein (1716), and Belgrade (1717), Austria becomes the leading power in the Danube area. Further territories are acquired by the Treaty of Karlowitz in 1699: (Turkish possessions in Hungary, Transylvania, and parts of Croatia and Slavonia), and by the Treaty of Passarowitz in 1718 (the Banat, northern Serbia, and parts of Wallachia and Bosnia).

Joseph Haydn

1695—
circa 1740

The heyday of Austrian Baroque, a product almost entirely of Austrian architects, such as Johann Bernhard Fischer von Erlach (1656—1723), Johann Lukas von Hildebrandt (1668—1745), Joseph Emanuel Fischer von Erlach (1693—1742), the Tyrolese Jakob Prandtauer (1660—1726), and the Court sculptor Meinrad Guggenbichler.

1714	By the Peace of Rastatt the Bourbons are promised Spain. Spanish territories in Italy and the Netherlands (Belgium) are acquired by Austria.
1717	Birth in the Vienna Hofburg of the Archduchess Maria Theresia, the last Habsburg ruler of genius, and founder of the Habsburg-Lothringen dynasty.
1732	The final act of the Counter-Reformation: Archbishop Firmian of Salzburg orders the expulsion of 20,000 Protestants.

Maria Theresia

1732	On March 31, at the tiny village of Rohrau on the Leitha, Lower Austria, Joseph Haydn, the creator of the classical symphony and master of the classical string quartet, was born.
1740—1763	In the War of the Austrian Succession (1740—1748) the Empress Maria Theresia resolutely defends her inheritance against the claims and attacks of Bavaria, Saxony, Prussia (Frederick the Great), and France. By the Treaty of Aachen she secures recognition of the Pragmatic Sanction, but is finally forced by the Treaty of Hubertusberg in 1763 to cede Silesia to Prussia.
1742—1780	Maria Theresia introduced many reforms, including the centralisation of the administration, the founding of the Military Academy, the reform of the army, compulsory education, and a new curriculum at the Vienna University, with lectures in German.

Joseph II

1744—1780	Among examples of Maria-Theresia Rococo are: Schönbrunn Palace, the Empress' favourite residence, built by Nicolaus Pacassi (1744—1760), with its French-style park and its menagerie by Nicolas Jadot (circa 1750); and the Residence at Innsbruck, with its allegorical ceiling frescoes by Franz Anton Maulpertsch (1776).
1756	On January 27 Wolfgang Amadeus Mozart, son of the Court Kapellmeister Leopold Mozart, was born at Salzburg.
Circa 1760—1800	Vienna becomes a centre of music and the theatre, as well as of Grand Opera (Orfeo, by Christoph Willibald Gluck 1762), Italian opera buffa, and the German "Singspiel" (Mozart's "Die Entführung" in 1781 and "Die Zauberflöte in 1791).
	The Emperor Joseph II founds the "Deutsches Nationaltheater Burgtheater" on the Michaelerplatz, Vienna, in 1776 and the Josefstädter Theater, the first "popular" theatre, in 1788.
1780—1790	Among the reforms introduced by the Emperor Joseph II were: abolition of serfdom, the Edict of Tolerance, special status for the Jews, civil marriage, dissolution of monasteries, and the secularisation of Church property.

19

1795	Austria, Russia, and Prussia agree on the Third Partition of Poland, by which Austria annexes West Galicia and Cracow, and acquires the Bukovina by an agreement with Turkey in 1775.

1797   By the Treaty of Campo Formio (First Coalition war) between the Emperor Franz I and the French Directoire Austria loses Belgium and receives in compensation Venetia, Istria, and Dalmatia.

1806   Dissolution of the Holy Roman Empire. The Emperor Franz renounces its crown following the declaration of sovereignty by the Confederation of the Rhine under pressure from Napoleon. Adoption of the title of "Emperor of Austria" in 1804.

Wolfgang Amadeus Mozart

1809   Vienna occupied by French troops. Napoleon's first defeat at the bloody battle of Aspern (May 20 1809). The new peace policy pursued by Fürst Clemens Metternich is consolidated by Napoleon's marriage to the Emperor's daughter Marie-Luise.

Tyrol, anno 1809. Tyrol's heroic fight for freedom against the French and Bavarian occupying forces. A national uprising led by Andreas Hofer of Passeiertal clears the enemy out of Tyrol after three victories at Berg Isel. On Austria's being compelled to cede Tyrol by the Peace of Schönbrunn, Andreas Hofer resumes hostilities on his own initiative, but has finally to yield to superior forces and on February 20 1810 is executed by the French at Mantua.

Andreas Hofer

1814—1815   The Congress of Vienna establishes a new order in Europe dominated by the Conservative eastern powers, Russia, Austria, and Prussia. The territorial decisions of the Congress include Austria's renunciation of the Habsburg Netherlands (Belgium), and of the Habsburg properties on the Upper Rhine, but her retention of Tyrol, Vorarlberg, Lombardy, and Venetia, as well as her acquisition of the recently (1803) secularised Archbishopric of Salzburg.

1815—1848

Ludwig van Beethoven

Fürst Clemens Metternich, the Austrian Chancellor and a leading European statesman of the day, presides over the destinies of the multi-racial Monarchy. At the centre of his "police State" is Vienna, an "intellectual Capua", the home of artists such as Ludwig van Beethoven (who lived and worked there from 1787 till his death in 1827), Franz Schubert, the first "Lieder" composer, and the waltz-kings Johann Strauss the Elder and Josef Lanner; the playwright and poet Franz Grillparzer, Ferdinand Raimund, with his popular pieces and fairy-stories, and Johann Nestroy, the popular actor and satirist. The leading lyricist of this "Biedermeier" age was Nikolaus Lenau, with Adalbert Stifter as the principal epic poet.

1820—1850	Opening of the first Austrian railway, the Kaiser-Ferdinand-Nordbahn, in 1839.
1848 March 13.—15.	Revolution in Vienna, the Liberals demanding the end of the detested Metternich regime. Resignation and flight of Metternich.
	April: Revolt in Hungary under Lajos Kossuth.
	October 6: The October Revolution in Vienna is put down by Field-Marshal Windischgrätz. Triumph of the Conservatives, and military dictatorship of Fürst Schwarzenberg. Abdication of the Emperor Ferdinand, who is succeeded by Franz Joseph I.
1848/49	The Risorgimento in Italy. Field-Marshal Radetzky's victories in northern Italy, followed by reassertion of Austrian authority.
1859—1869	Expansion of Vienna's city boundaries and razing of the bastions. Founding of the first great banks and of a free Press ("Neue Freie Presse"). Formation of the Social-democratic party in 1868.
1859—1866	Unification of Italy. Sardinia and their French allies defeat the Austrians at Magenta and Solferino. Austria loses Lombardy and Venetia (1866).
1866	End of the Austro-Prussian condominium. Following her defeat by Prussia at Sadowa Austria loses the hegemony of the German Confederation. Bismarck's astute policy of clemency refrains from imposing a territorial indemnity on Austria.
1873	World Exhibition in Vienna. The economic crisis leads to a slump on the Stock Exchange, and the failure of 125 new banks.

Anton Bruckner

1856—1890

Franz Schubert

Vienna takes on the appearance of an Imperial capital: completion of the Ringstrasse.

The Age of Imperialism.

The Vienna of to-day takes shape, with the monumental buildings of Heinrich von Ferstel (the Votivkirche 1856—1879); the University; the Opera House by Siccardsburg and van der Nüll, opened in 1869; the Court Museums, Hofburgtheater, and new wing of the Hofburg by Semper and Hasenauer; the new Rathaus and the church of Maria vom Siege by Friedrich Schmid. Ceremonial statuary by Anton Fernkorn (the equestrian statues of the Archduke Karl and Prince Eugene); by Kaspar von Zumbusch (statues of the Empress Maria Theresia, Field-Marshal Radetzky, and Ludwig van Beethoven); and by Friedrich Helmer (Athene in front of the Parliament).

History	Culture

Circa 1860—1900

Music composed in Vienna includes the works of the last of the classical symphonists Johannes Brahms, who made Vienna his home from 1878 till his death in 1897; of the one-time organist at the monastery of St. Florian, Anton Bruckner; and of the master of classical operetta, Johann Strauss the Younger.

1900—1917

In the realm of science and technology, Julius von Wagner-Jauregg developed his epoch-making theory of the countering of progressive paralysis by malaria treatment (1917); and Sigmund Freud, the pioneer of psychoanalysis, published his theory of the origins of neuroses (1900).

Johann Strauss the Younger

1914—1918

June 1914; murder at Sarajevo of the heir to the Austrian throne, Archduke Franz Ferdinand, and his morganatic wife Duchess Sophie von Hohenburg.

July 28 1914; Austria declares war on Serbia and enters World War I at the side of her ally Germany.

October 1918; dissolution of the Dual Monarchy and creation of the "Successor States" (Czechoslovakia, Hungary, Yugoslavia, and Austria).

1918

November 11; the last Emperor, Karl, renounces all his royal prerogatives. Proclamation in front of the Parliament building of the first Austrian republic.

1919

By the Treaty of St. Germain the tiny Austrian Republic has to assume responsibility for the policy of the Habsburg Monarchy and cede all South Tyrol south of the Brenner Pass to Italy, as well as one or two areas in Lower Austria to Czechoslovakia.

Franz Joseph I

1919—1920

Defensive operations against Yugoslav incursions, and a plebiscite in the areas of Carinthia occupied by Yugoslav forces, secure the province's retention by Austria. Inflation is mastered by the brilliant financial policy of Chancellor Ignaz Seipel.

EISENSTADIVM
vulgo EISNSTAT, in vltimis finibus Austriæ Inferioris ciuitas.

Eisenstadt 1618

1932—1934	Economic crisis in Austria. Frequent disturbances and occasional pitched battles between Marxist and National-Socialist armed formations. Dissolution of the National Assembly by Chancellor Dollfuss and banning of political parties. Foundation of the "Fatherland Front".
1934	July 25. Failure of a National-Socialist "putsch" in Vienna. Murder of Chancellor Dollfuss.
1938	March 13. Adolf Hitler occupies Austria and forcibly incorporates it in the "Third Reich". Vienna sinks to the status of provincial capital of the "Ostmark". The name "Austria" is "officially deleted from the map".
1939—1945	World War II draws to an end with the defeat of the German army at Stalingrad (1942/43) and the landing of British and American forces in Normandy (June 6 1944). Final defeat and capitulation of Germany.
1944	April 12. The first bombs fall in the area of "Greater Vienna".
1945	April 2. The Danube bridges blown up by SS troops. During the last days of the fighting in Vienna the Burgtheater and St. Stephen's Cathedral were destroyed by artillery fire. A month previously the Opera had been destroyed in an air-raid.
1945	April 13. Vienna falls to the Red Army after a five-day siege. The Austrian provinces are occupied by British, French, American, and Russian troops.

1945   April 27. Formation of a Provisional Government in Vienna under Chancellor Renner.

1945   April 27—May 10. The first post-war (Philharmonic) concert in the Grosser Musikvereinssaal in Vienna. The Vienna Burgtheater, playing in the Ronacher Theatre, re-opens with Grillparzer's "Sappho". The State Opera (Director Raoul Aslan) gives a performance of "Figaro" in the Volksoper. Opening of the University and high-schools.

1945   July 4. Restitution of the Austrian Republic based on the Constitution of 1927.

    Franz Lehár, the famous composer of Viennese Operetta, dies in Bad Ischl.

1957   Vienna divided into 4 sectors, and the provinces into 4 zones, of occupation.

Bad Ischl

1945/46   Vienna goes hungry: normal weekly ration 888 calories. The UNRRA famine relief scheme.

1945/55   Reconstruction of St. Stephen's Cathedral by the Cathedral architect Holey. Reconstruction of the Opera to a design by Erich Boltenstern. Housing programme set on foot with international aid schemes.

1955   May 15. Signature of the Austrian State Treaty in the Marmorsaal of the Belvedere Palace by the Foreign Ministers of Great Britain, France, Russia, and the USA, and by the Austrian Foreign Minister Leopold Figl.

1955   October 25. The last soldier of the occupation forces leaves Austrian soil. Vienna is chosen as the seat of the International Atomic Energy Agency.

The State Opera House, Vienna

THE PICTURES

(Frontispiece) The Vordere Gosausee in the Salzkammergut, is one of the loveliest beauty-spots in the Austrian Alps. Behind the great rocky wall of the Torstein is the Dachstein massif. The glacier shining like a beacon above the valley is the Gosau glacier.

(33) One of the finest examples of baroque art in Austria is the Upper Belvedere Palace in Vienna built by Johann Lukas von Hildebrandt for Prince Eugene of Savoy. The wrought-iron park gates (1721—1723) are by Arnold and Konrad Küffner (1728). The Upper Belvedere was the Court residence of Franz Ferdinand, the heir to the Austrian throne who was murdered at Sarajevo in 1914.

(34) The Ringstrasse in Vienna, which is over 3 miles long, boasts several fine buildings, including the Parliament (1873—1883), a hellenistic building by Theophil Hansen, and the neo-gothic Rathaus (1872—1883) by the architect Friedrich von Schmidt.

(35) That Vienna is a "garden city" can be seen from this aerial photograph with its pattern of green islands set in a sea of houses. It is almost as if the Vienna Woods were lapping up against the city centre so as to set off, and slightly relieve, the monumental dignity of the Parliament, the Rathaus, and the Burgtheater.

(36) With the Turkish menace finally disposed of, work was begun on the Palace of Schönbrunn on the outskirts of Vienna in 1695/96 to a design by Johann Bernhard Fischer von Erlach. Particularly attractive is the Park with the Gloriette, completed in 1775, on top of the hill. The Palace was the summer residence of the Habsburgs from Maria Theresia's time onwards, and it was here that Franz Joseph I died in 1916.

(37) Entering the Belvedere Palace, built for Austria's most illustrious military commander, Prince Eugene of Savoy, the first room one comes to is the Sala Terrena, the ceiling of which is supported by four overlife-size figures of Atlas. As in all the ceremonial apartments designed by Hildebrandt, this low-ceilinged vestibule (1721—1723) contains an exuberant profusion of baroque stucco decoration, in this case by Claude le Fort du Plessy.

(38) The name "Graben" comes from the filled-in artificial moat of the one-time Roman camp of Vindobona, established in 16 B..C. The stone column, a masterpiece of high baroque combining architecture and sculpture designed by Burnacini, illustrates various theological motifs. The Emperor Leopold I had it erected here in the Graben as a votive offering in gratitude for deliverance from the plague and from the Turkish menace of 1683.

(39) The most important ecclesiastical high baroque building in Austria is the Karlskirche in Vienna. The site on which Johann Bernhard Fischer von Erlach's masterpiece stands was originally outside the city walls. In this stately church with its massive dome the facade blends perfectly with the central structure, and a number of different architectural styles are harmoniously combined.

(40/41) Opposite the Rathaus is the late Italian Renaissance Burgtheater. In the background can be seen a number of Vienna's most prominent buildings, including St. Stephen's Cathedral.

(42) Silver ware in the Hofburg, Vienna. The table laid for a ceremonial banquet in the older wing of the Hofburg, containing the Studies of the Emperors Franz Joseph and Karl, gives some idea of one-time Court ceremonial.

(43) The first stage in the development of the new Ringstrasse was the building of the Opera House between 1861 and 1869, based on plans by August von Siccardsburg and Eduard van der Null. The Vienna Opera might be called the Mecca of the operatic world, and among its directors have been composers such as Gustav Mahler and Richard Strauss. The original house was destroyed in 1945, but its restoration by Erich Boltenstern is one of the finest examples of theatrical reconstruction in Europe.

(44) The Spanish Riding-school in the Hofburg, founded by Karl VI, soon became the most important centre of "haute école." The building in which Austria's world-famous equestrian ballet go through their paces has been preserved in the original classicistic style of Josef Emmanuel Fischer von Erlach. The picture shows one of the high-lights of the programme, the "Courbette an der Hand."

(45) "The Heldenplatz is not a square but a langscape . . . It is the stage on which the Ringstrasse puts on its most fascinating show, the triumph and apotheosis of ensemble." This was how one Viennese reacted to this great open space in front of the Hofburg, containing the two equestrian statues of Prince Eugene and the Archduke Karl, who defeated Napoleon at Aspern. In the background is the tower of the Rathaus.

(46) At the very heart of Vienna, pointing up into the sky "like the finger of God" is the 560 feet high tower of St. Stephen's Cathedral. The Cathedral, which is some 340 feet in length, can trace its origins back to the 13th century. The gothic tower was completed in 1433. The roof was destroyed by fire during the last weeks of World War II, as was the vaulted roof of the choir. The "Pummerin," the Cathedral's largest bell, was also shattered. After the war the restoration of the Cathedral was immediately put in hand, funds being contributed by all classes and sections of the Austrian people.

(47) The chancel of St. Stephen's Cathedral in Vienna, with its busts of the four Fathers of the Church, dates from 1515 and is one of the masterpieces of the ecclesiastical architect Anton Pilgram.

(48) The Stadium in the Prater, which holds 90,000 spectators, was opened in 1931 and enlarged in 1959. The park-like Prater provides an attractive setting.

(49) "Dedicated to the youth of Vienna and to men of goodwill the world over as a centre of friendly competition in the Arts and in sport." So runs the inscription at the entrance to the Stadthalle in Vienna. Designed by Roland Rainer (1954—1958) the Stadthalle is Europe's most modern indoor arena.

(50) Baden bei Wien is situated at the western end of the series of hot curative springs that were known as long ago as Roman times. In fact, Baden's reputation as a spa goes back thousands of years. One of its chief attractions is the lovely park, where visitors can find ease and relaxation beneath trees that have survived many an age of destruction.

(51) The pretty little village of Gumpoldskirchen, near Vienna, famous for its wines, was a parish as long ago as 1235. As well as one or two mediaeval buildings it can point to a number of houses from the 16th and 17th centuries still in excellent preservation. Gumpoldskirchen is seen at its best at vintage time.

(52) The moated castle of Heidenreichstein in the north-west corner of Lower Austria owes its present grim, forbidding aspect to alterations carried out to the original 13th century building by the Puchheim family during the 15th century, including the erection of massive towers at three corners. In the background can be seen the 13th century rectanlugar keep.

(53) On the top of a sheer wall of rock rising a thousand feet above the Danube are the ruins of Aggstein, dating from 1100—1113. Many stories are told of Aggstein; marauders came and went, and in 1529 it was burnt down by the Turks. It was after the Thirty Year's War that the castle began to go to ruin. To-day, Aggstein is the most famous ruined castle in Lower Austria.

(54) The Cistercian Monastery of Heiligenkreuz in the southern part of the Vienna Woods is one of the oldest centres of culture in Austria. As well as for its romantic surroundings, the monastery is notable for its fine cloisters (1220—1250).

(55) Austria has a wealth of objets d'art quite apart from what is to be found in the museums of Vienna and the provincial capitals. The late gothic triptych-altar in the 15th century parish church of Maria Laach, Lower Austria, partly carved and partly painted, is by a unknown Passau master of about 1500.

(56) The little village of Melk, founded about 976 by the Babenberg Emperor Leopold I, has become famous for its Benedictine monastery, one of the great architectural masterpieces of the western world. It is here that the Danube landscape culminates in this architectural miracle built on a rock jutting out into the Danube. Even the Autobahn passing the village by in an elegant curve seems to keep a respectful distance from the monastery, as if in homage to Baroque!

(57) In the 11th century the present Benedictine establishment at Melk was a fortified monastery. In its present form it is the work of the Tyrolese sculptor and architect Jakob Prandtauer, who early in the 18th century was called upon to execute a project the like of which Austria had never known before. Important features in the general effect are the symmetry of the whole and the way it blends so harmoniously with the Danube landscape.

(58) Originally held in feudal tenure by the bishopric of Passau, Schloss Schönbühel, at the entrance to the Wachau, later passed into the possession of the Counts von Starhemberg, who founded a Servite monastery here. In the reconstruction of the Schloss to its present form in the 19th century, bricks from the original walls were used. There is a pleasing simplicity about the building.

(59) The Augustinian monastery of St. Florian is the finest example of the spirit of baroque, as exemplified in architecture, in Upper Austria. The world-famous staircase (1706—1716) was originally designed by Jakob Prandtauer, who has executed a masterly adaptation of a plan by the highly talented Milanese Carlone.

(60) The most undulating part of Upper Austria is the "Mühlviertel" north of the Danube. Near the market town of Neufelden to the northwest of Linz the hydro-electric power station of Partenstein is served by a reservoir that makes a harmonious contribution to the undulating landscape.

(61) The tower at Enns, Upper Austria, is a detached construction four stories high, and was erected in 1564 on a spacious rectangular square to serve as a clock- and watchtower. Though there is something Gothic about the details of the massive stone prisms, the general aspect of the tower is Renaissance. It sets off most strikingly the severe horizontal lines of the square.

(62) Steyr, at the confluence of the rivers Enns and Steyr, is the second-largest and the most beautiful town in Upper Austria. At every step the visitor comes upon Gothic and

Baroque walls and monuments, and the oblong main square is surrounded by rows of flat-fronted houses with pointed gables. From earliest times Steyr has been the place where iron is brought from the Erzberg down the river Enns to be manufactured and exported all over the world. Apart from its mediaeval and Romantic monuments Steyr is also the home of the Steyr-Daimler-Puch Company, on which the present prosperity of the former iron-centre is largely based. Steyr has always remained faithful to iron and has had no cause to regret it.

(63) The skyline of the Upper Austrian capital of Linz is a jumble of baroque towers, factory chimneys, and steel-foundries, yet Linz, the Roman Lentia, remains a pleasant city in rural surroundings on the right bank of the Danube. Amid the sea of houses the Landstrasse, the principal shopping street, is clearly discernible. To the south of the city are the Austrian Nitrogen works and the famous Linz-Donawitz LD-steel works known as VOEST.

(64) Between the rounded peaks of the Schieferalpen, with the Schmittenhöhe in the west and the Hundstein in the east is the Zeller See, one of the most beautiful lakes in the Alps. Situated on a slight elevation on its western shore is the resort of Zell am See, with a parish church first mentioned in the 8th century. The peak reflected in the placid surface of the lake is the Kitzsteinhorn (9,570 feet), in the Hohe Tauern range.

(65) The two lakes in the Styrian part of the Salzkammergut are the Toplitzsee and the Grundlsee. It was at Toplitzsee (foreground) that Archduke Johann first met the girl he later married, the postman's daughter Anna Plochl. On the eastern shore of the Grundlsee, Styria's largest lake, is Gössl, a paradise for campers. In the background is the Sarstein, 6,520 feet.

(66) There is something of the South about Gmunden at the north end of the Traunsee. The Esplanade runs as far as Schloss Orth, built partly on land and partly on water. The lakeside wing was rebuilt in its present form after a fire in 1634. One of its most prominent features is the massive "onion" cupola above the gateway.

(67) There is a magic quality about the Traunsee. The rays of the morning sun lighting on the fishing-nets hung out to dry make them look like gossamer flags of silver tissue hoisted in honour of a lovely day to come.

(68) The torrent roaring through the gorge of Bad Gastein cascades in two marvellous waterfalls of 200 and 280 feet. The steep mountain-slopes on either side of the raging torrent are dominated by the lofty hotels of this world-famous resort. The highly radio-active water piped into the hotels and pump-rooms from 18 curative springs is taken medicinally or in the form of baths and is extremely successful in the treatment of nervous disorders, gout and rheumatic complaints. The first doctor and naturalist to explore the healing possibilities of the springs of Bad Gastein was Paracelsus in 1562. Bad Gastein is also a famous winter-sports resort, the Stubnerkogel cable railway giving access to extensive skiing slopes on the western side of the valley and a wonderful variety of mountain walks in the Tauern.

(69) The air is full of the sound of cowbells; the clouds drift slowly over the limestone crags of the Dachstein massif; and amid the peace of the mountains a happy woman goes about her daily work. As she works she smiles, for she feels at one with the serenity of the high sun-blest pastures.

(70) Salzburg, one of Europe's most beautiful cities, lies at the entrance of one of the most important gateways to the Alps. The city is a jewel of mediaeval, and particularly of ecclesiastical, architecture. The mediaeval mass of the Hohensalzburg Fortress dominates the city from its Mönchsberg fastness 400 feet above the river Salzach. At its feet, on the left bank of the river, are the Old Town and the Cathedral, built on the site of a church first consecrated in 774, and completed (1614—1628) by Santino Solari in monumental early baroque style. The dome was destroyed in an air-raid in 1944, but has been restored.

(71) Not far from Salzburg is the neo-gothic Schloss Anif. It was here that King Ludwig III of Bavaria abdicated after World War I.

(72) The Mirabell Gardens in Salzburg, with their marble statues, clipped hedges, and flower-beds are a lovely example of Austrian baroque garden-design. They were laid out for ceremonial open-air occasions by (probably) Johann Bernhard Fischer von Erlach at the time of Archbishop Johann Ernst Thun (1687—1709). The Hohensalzburg Castle provides a most effective background.

(73) The hub of the Old Town in Salzburg is the spacious Residenzplatz with its fountain, a monumental design of Untersberg marble, executed by an Italian artist between 1656 and 1661.

(74) From the Nonnberg Benedictine Convent in Salzburg there is a charming view of the domes of St. Erhard's church, built in baroque style by Caspar Zugalli (1685—1689).

(75) The country palace at Hellbrunn near Salzburg was built in gay early baroque style (1613—1615) by Santino Solari for Archbishop Marcus Sitticus. The garden, with its fountains and aquatic jokes, is laid out in Italian style and is the oldest German baroque garden in existence.

(76) Farmsteads like this have been a feature of the Salzburg landscape for centuries; their shingle-roofs are surmounted by a little tower with a bell to call the workers in the fields to their meals. Dominating the scene is the 9,700 foot Hochkönig.

(77) The waterfall at Krimml, Salzburg, drops 1,250 feet in three stages, the first stage being a perpendicular drop of

460 feet. A protruding rock interrupts the last stage. The whole forms a magnificent spectacle, unique in the Eastern Alps.

(78) The Gross Glockner, 12,530 feet, is the highest mountain in Austria. To climb it from the Franz-Josephs Haus or from Heiligenblut means taking in en route the Klein Glockner, 12,440 feet, which can be seen in this picture.

(79) One of the most impressive hydro-electric plants in Europe is the giant Glockner-Kaprun station in the Hohe Tauern range. The water is collected in the "Mooserboden" (background) and "Wasserfallboden" reservoirs. The Limberg dam across the latter contains 86 million cubic metres of water, the same capacity as the "Mooserboden" reservoir formed by the "Mooser" and the "Drossen" dams (in the middle of the picture).

(80) The Stubai Alps are some of the loftiest in the whole central range of the Eastern Alps, with several peaks of over 10,000 feet and a number of gleaming glaciers, known in West Tyrol dialect as "Ferner." One of the ice-clad Stubai giants is reflected in the waters of the Rinnensee.

(81) The way back to the ice-age has been made very simple for to-day's traveller: all he has to do is to take a ticket on the Dachstein cable railway and join a conducted party at the Dachsteinhöhlenhaus, and he will see vast caves with cascades of stalactites. The fairy-tale world of these ice-caves is one of Austria's greatest tourist attractions.

(82) The rugged ridge of the south face of the Wilder Kaiser group, Tyrol, is a magnificent wall of rock, a section of the northern part of the Austrian limestone Alps. The face drops perpendicularly into an extensive basin, in which are situated the villages of St. Johann and Ellmau.

(83) Over the lively frontier-town of Kufstein lowers the fortress of Geroldseck. When the Emperor Maximilian acquired the districts of Kitzbühel, Kufstein, and Rattenberg for Tyrol, he had to bring up artillery to reduce Geroldseck in 1504. The fortress contains a giant organ that plays daily in commemoration of the dead of two World Wars.

(84) Sheep-breeding is an important part of peasant life in the Ötztal, Tyrol. The last outposts of the farmer in the high mountains are the pastures high above the tree-line.

(85) The silver and copper miners of the Kitzbühel of about 1500 would be amazed if they could see this snug little town to-day. Though it still retains something of its mediaeval character, the miners of those days have given way to the skiers who have made Kitzbühel the "winter capital" of Austria. It is bounded to the south by the Kitzbüheler Schieferalpen, which are grass-covered right up to their summits. The town was given its charter by Duke Ludwig II in 1271.

(86) In 1218 Hugo I of Montfort presented the Order of the Knights of St. John with various properties in the Klostertal on condition that travellers over the Arlberg were provided with fire, water, and accommodation in the "Stuben," special mountain huts. It is to them that the present village of Stuben in Vorarlberg, which can be regarded as the cradle of Arlberg skiing, owes its origin.

(87) Tyrol's extensive forests mean a flourishing timber trade, comprising nearly 600 firms. Lumbermen in Tyrol are never out of work. In the background is the Wilder Kaiser group from the south.

(88) The "Goldene Dachl" in Innsbruck. In 1500 the Emperor Maximilian I ordered a late-gothic balcony roofed with gilded copper tiles to be added to the new Court residence, so providing a place from which the Court could watch ceremonial processions, etc. The sandstone reliefs and heraldic devices on the exterior are the work of Nikolaus Türing the Elder, and depict some of the artists and comedians that used to take part in the pageants watched by the Court from the "Goldene Dachl."

(89) The Maria Theresien Strasse in Innsbruck is considered one of the world's most beautiful streets, in which architecture and Nature combine to form an unforgettable picture. The baroque column in the middle, the "Annasäule," commemorates the withdrawal of enemy troops from Innsbruck on St. Anne's Day 1703.

(90) The Karwendel range, stretching from Scharnitz to Achensee and from the Inn valley to the Isar, comprises about 900 square kilometres of mountain solitude. Climbers and walkers alike extol the wild beauty of its remote valleys, its grim inaccessible walls of rock, and the brilliant green of the "Ahornboden", a miraculous oasis of cultivation amid a sea of stones.

(91) On September 13, 1959 there was a parade in Innsbruck of more than 20,000 levies in original costume, giving the 100,000 spectators some idea of the intensity of Tyrolese patriotism. The Zillertal levies in the picture are the descendants of those who fought with Andreas Hofer at Berg Isel in 1809.

(92) From Mayrhofen in the Zillertal the Penken cable railway leads to a paradise of high pastures and mountain solitude whence the eye ranges over the canyon-like Zillertal to the peaks and glaciers of the Zillertal Alps.

(93) The Fernpass is one of the loveliest roads in Tyrol, with a series of idyllic lakes nestling amid an Alpine landscape of heroic grandeur. The Fernpass road runs from the sunny little town of Imst up to the Zugspitze neighbourhood and the resorts of Lermoos and Ehrwald.

(94) The church-tower of Leiblfing in the Upper Inn valley with its tapering spire was built in 1710. For over 900 years there has been a church of one kind or another on this hill. The road at its foot is Austria's main highway, the Vienna—Bregenz road.

(95) In Tyrol, dairy-farming is second only to forestry in importance. The cattle pass the summer on high mountain pastures which provide excellent fodder.

(96) At the turn of the 13th and 14th centuries emigrants from Canton Valais in Switzerland formed a scattered settlement at Lech, in Vorarlberg, on the banks of the river Lech not far from its source. The houses are still scattered all over the valley and the foothills in typical Valais fashion. During the present century Lech has become famous as an international skiing resort.

(97) The sunburnt wooden houses of Alpbach, near Brixlegg in Tyrol, form a compact, intimate world of their own. In August and September students, scientists, scholars, and politicians from all over the world assemble here for a Course organised by the "Österreichisches College" in furtherance of European co-operation.

(98) In Tyrol, the cattle spend the summer at high altitudes where in spite of every modern improvement known to dairy-farming the pastures, with the high mountains in the background, still preserve an atmosphere of natural serenity.

(99) The little village of Innerberg, prominently situated 3,800 feet above sea-level against the background of the Rätikon massif, is on the right-hand side of the entrance to the Silbertal in Montafon, Vorarlberg, where silver-ore was mined from the days of the Fuggers until 1570. Montafon's present prosperity is derived not from silver but from the so-called "white gold," the electric power generated by the vast "Illwerk" plants. Montafon exports electric power right up to the industrial area of north-west Germany.

(100) The church at Lech, with its massive tower, originally dates from the 14th and 15th centuries, with 18th century baroque additions. It is a characteristic landmark of the original Valais settlement.

(101) Seefeld, Tyrol, is situated on a sunny saddle 4,000 feet above sea-level over which run the road and railway from Mittenwald to Innsbruck. It is one of Tyrol's most popular ski resorts and in 1964 will be the venue of the winter Olympic Games. The round chapel in the picture was completed in 1628.

(102) Zürs on the Arlberg; the skiers' Mecca, with every conceivable amenity including a wealth of ski-lifts to the magnificent higher slopes and a winter season that sometimes lasts till mid-May. Zürs is reached via the Arlberg and Flexen passes.

(103) South of Nenzing in Vorarlberg are the extensive Gamperdone pastures and forests, with an abundance of game. The narrow Walgau, remote from the bustle and clamour of modern civilisation, has justly earned the title of "the Nenzing Paradise."

(104) Feldkirch in Vorarlberg was originally a stronghold dominated by the Schattenburg, the seat of the Counts of Mont-fort. Dating from the first half of the 12th century, the Schattenburg is the largest and best-preserved castle in Vorarlberg. There is still a mediaeval atmosphere about the narrow alleys and arcades of Feldkirch.

(105) Bregenz is the capital of the province of Vorarlberg. Between the "local" mountain, Pfänder, and the shore of Lake Constance is a narrow strip of land known as the "Klause," on which the Celtic-Roman settlement of Brigantium came into being, controlling the road to the south. Its strategic importance has involved Bregenz in the ravages of war more frequently than any other town in Vorarlberg. To-day it boasts one of Austria's most colourful summer Festivals, with its famous "floating stage" productions. The cable-railway to the top of Pfänder (3,500 feet), completed in 1927, affords an incomparable panorama.

(106) From the summit of a sheer rock, originally a fortified site, the pilgrimage church of "Mariä Heimsuchung" in Rankweil, Vorarlberg, has a superb view over the Rhine valley. The oldest part of the church dates from the 15th century. Much older than the "Burg Gottes" on the Frauenberg is the little Peterskirche, first mentioned in 830. In the background are the Swiss mountains on the far side of the Rhine.

(107) The cable-railway up Valluga at St. Anton am Arlberg is one of Austria's most spectacular cable railways. From the top of the Galzig railway (6,865 feet) it goes up to the summit of Valluga (9,276 feet) on the border between Tyrol and Vorarlberg. The view from the summit is virtually limitless. The picture shows the view westwards with the Pazielfernerspitze and Scesaplana.

(108) The 30 Miles long Grossglockner road from Bruck in Salzburg to Heiligenblut in Carinthia is one of Europe's most magnificent roads, and of incomparable scenic grandeur. It includes two branch-roads, one of which, 5 miles long, leads up to the Franz-Josephs-Höhe (7,820 feet), where motorists from all over the world stop to enjoy the view over the Pasterze glacier of the Grossglockner (12,330 feet), Austria's highest mountain.

(109) The Wörther See near Klagenfurt in Carinthia is the warmest of the larger Alpine lakes with summer temperatures of up to 75 degrees F. Along the 10 mile length of its shores are a string of popular resorts, idyllic villages, and excellent golf-courses. Among the best-known resorts are Krumpendorf, Pörtschach, and Velden. This colour photograph was taken from the bathing-beach at Velden.

(110) Carinthia abounds in wayside shrines, some of which are centuries old, but this one belongs to the internal combustion age. The shingle-roof over the Frescoes points to Heaven in a reminder to the motorist that at all times his life is in God's hands.

(111) The parish church of Maria Wörth was built on a small peninsular jutting out into the Wörther See towards the middle

of the 12th century. Originally it was the property of the Bishop of Freising. The actual settlement is first mentioned in the 9th century. The chapel adjoining the church contains some valuable 12th century Frescoes.

(112) The shores of the Wörther See are Austria's "Riviera," and for the citizens of Klagenfurt, lucky people, it is only a few miles journey to the gay life of its international resorts.

(113) On the site formerly occupied by the 13th century castle is the Klagenfurt "Landhaus," dating from the second half of the 16th century. It is built in the shape of a horse-shoe, and the courtyard is definitely Renaissance in character, with its two towers and shady colonnades.

(114) The hill-top church of Maria Saal, the oldest place of Christian worship in Carinthia, has been surrounded by defensive ramparts since the 15th century. The picture shows the Gothic watch-tower, the lower part of which originally served as a charnel-house. The late-Gothic shrine with its graceful little lantern-tower was set up in 1497.

(115). The majestic castle of Hochosterwitz occupies a conspicuous site on a precipitous rock, and is one of Carinthia's most famous landmarks. It is first mentioned in documents from the year 860; later Georg Khevenhüller (1533—1587) converted it into a fortress with 14 massive gateways and a series of bastions, making masterly use of all the defensive advantages of the sheer rock on which it stands. This view of the castle is from the south-west.

(116) The Riegersburg, Styria's largest castle, dominating the market-town of the same name from its commanding position on a sheer basalt rock, was a bulwark against the Turks. From the inner courtyard, reached by way of seven gateways and two moats, there is a superb panorama in the direction of the Yugoslav frontier.

(117) Graz, Austria's second largest city and the capital of Styria, consisted in the Middle Ages of a single large square, the present Hauptplatz, where the only two arcaded houses in Graz are to be found; the Luegghaus, dating from the early 16th century, and its neighbour from 1691. In the background can be seen the Schlossberg and the well-known clock, which originally formed part of the defensive works; in its present form it dates from 1561, and was only provided with a clock-face in 1712.

(118) The double spiral staircase in the Burg at Graz dates from the reconstruction of the Burg by the Emperor Maximilian I between 1494 and 1500. It is a fine testimony to the originality and skill of late mediaeval craftmanship.

(119) The Benedictine monastery of Admont in the Ennstal, Styria, founded in 1074, was burnt down in 1865, but the library, a masterpiece executed by Gotthard Hayberger of Steyr at the time of Abbot Anton II of Mainersberg (1718—1751) survived. Modelled on the Austrian National Library in Vienna, it measures 70 metres in length but is only 13 metres wide. In the cupola-like vaulting lit by 60 windows are some fine allegorical Frescoes by Bartolomeo Altomonte executed in 1774.

(120) On the rushing river Salza, a tributary of the Enns, canoe races are held every year. Formerly the river was an important means of timber transport.

(121) The Neusiedler See in Burgenland, 220 square miles in area, with a length of 22 miles, a width of 3 to 5 miles, and an average depth of only 5 feet, is surrounded by an extensive border of reeds, a sanctuary for all kinds of water-fowl. This large expanse of water acts as a deterrent to frost and makes for mild autumns, so that the vineyards and orchards on its western shore enjoy an ideal climate. It is also a favourite place for sailing and ice-sailing.

(122/123) The cutting and processing of reeds is an important industry in Burgenland.

(124) Burg Forchtenstein, south-west of Mattersburg in Burgenland, lived its finest hour in 1683 when the Grand Vizier Kara Mustafa at the head of a mighty host swept up to the gates of Vienna. Of all the border castles and strongholds only Forchtenstein held out. This superbly situated castle is crowned by a massive round tower from the late 13th century. To-day the castle provides a spectacular setting for open-air performances of classical dramas.

(125) The spirit of Joseph Haydn pervades Eisenstadt, Burgenland's capital, from end to end; in the elaborate Esterházy Palace, in his modest little house (which is now a museum containing a wealth of interesting and valuable material) and in the mausoleum where he was laid to rest.

(126) "E'en as a tiddler I played with pigs": the words of the old song can be aptly applied to almost any peasant in Burgenland, where pigbreeding, especially east of the Neusiedler See, is an important source of income.

(127) To the east of the Neusiedler See and still on Austrian soil are the beginnings of the great Hungarian plain stretching away into the limitless distance, a typically eastern European landscape dotted here und there with warm salty tarns. In summer places like St. Andrä near Frauenkirchen enjoy a climate comparable with that of Heluan in Egypt. The only vertical lines in all the wide open spaces are the poles of the wells.

(128) The Neusiedler See is a place of mystery: nobody even knows where it derives its water from. Actually it should by rights have dried up years ago, for condensation accounts for more than four times the amount of water it receives from the tiny river Wulka. In fact "Vienna's lake," as it is sometimes called, does dry up about once in a century, but the water always comes back, stealthily and mysteriously. Truly a baffling phenomenon, the Neusiedler See.

INDEX OF PHOTOGRAPHERS

Wien. *Südfront und Haupttor des Oberen Belvedere*
Vienna. South front and main entrance at the Upper Belvedere Palac
La façade Sud et l'entrée principale du Belvédère, Vienn

32

ien. Parlament
enna. Parliament
enne. Parlement

Luftaufnahme. Parlament, Rathaus, Burgtheater
Air view of the city. Parliament, Rathaus, Burgtheater
Vienne à vol d'oiseau: Parlement, Hôtel de Ville, Burgtheater

35

loß Schönbrunn in Wien
önbrunn Palace, Vienna
château de Schönbrunn à Vienne

Gartensaal im Oberen Belvedere in Wien
Garden Room in the Upper Belvedere, Vienna
La salle du jardin du Belvédère supérieur à Vienne

37

...säule auf dem Graben, Wien
...Holy Trinity Column, called the Plague Column, on the Graben, Vienna
...onne votive érigée après une épidémie de peste, sur le Graben à Vienne

Die Karlskirche, Wien
The Karlskirche, Vienna
Karlskirche, Vienne

Blick auf Wien
View of Vienna
Une vue de Vienne

Festtafel in der Hofburg, Wien
Gala dinner in the Hofburg, Vienna
Une table pour un dîner de gala, de la Hofburg, Vienne

Galaabend in der Op
Gala Performance in the State Opera House, Vien
Soirée de gala à l'Opéra de Vienn

42

Courbette an der Hand. Die Spanische Reitschule in der Hofburg
The Spanish Riding School in the Hofburg, Vienna
Hofburg, le manège de l'Ecole espagnole

Wien, der Heldenpla
Vienna, the Heldenplatz in front of the Hofbu
Vienne, Place des Héros devant la Hofbu

44

adion der Stadt Wien
adium, Vienna
Stade de Vienne

Radrennen in der Stadthalle in Wien
Bicycle race in the Stadthalle, Vienna
Au vélodrome dans la Hall municipal

49

Kurpark in Baden bei Wien
Park in the health-resort of Baden, near Vienna
Un parc de la station de cure de Baden, près de Vienne

Weinernte mit Blick auf Gumpoldskirch
Vineyards near Gumpoldskirch
Les vendanges près de Gumpoldskirch

Schloß Heidenreichstein, N.-Ö., eine Wasserburg
The moated castle of Heidenreichstein, Lower Austria
Le château de Heidenreichstein, Basse-Autriche

Die Ruine Aggstein in der Wachau, N.-
The ruins of Aggstein. Wachau, Lower Aust
Les ruines du château d'Aggstein, Wachau, Basse-Autric

Kreuzgang des Stiftes Heiligenkreuz, N.-Ö.
Cloister of the Monastery of Heiligenkreuz, Lower Austria
Le cloître du monastère de Heiligenkreuz, Basse-Autriche

Ausschnitt aus dem spätgotischen Doppelflügelaltar in Maria La
Select of the late gothic triptych-altar of Maria La
Fragment du retable de Maria La

Autostraße bei Stift Melk, N.-Ö.
Autobahn near the monastery of Melk, Lower Austria
Autoroute près du monastère de Melk, Basse-Autriche

Stift Me
The monastery of Me
Le monastère de Me

Stausee bei Neufelden in Oberösterreich
Dam at Neufelden, Upper Austria
Le lac de barrage de Neufelden, Haute-Autriche

Aus der zum Schutze erbauten Ennsburg entstand die Stadt En
The city of Enns grew up around the fortress of Ennsbu
La ville d'Enns se développa au pied de sa forteres

Die Eisenstadt Steyr ist eine der schönsten Städte Österreichs
Steyr is one of the most beautiful towns in Austria
Steyr, la ville du fer, est l'une des plus belles villes d'Autriche

Linz, die Landeshauptstadt Oberösterre.
Linz, capital of Upper Aus
Linz, capitale de la Haute-Autr

r Zeller See vor der Glocknergruppe
ller See at the foot of the Glockner Group
lac du Zell devant la chaîne du Glockner

Das Salzkammergut. Toplitzsee, Gößl am Grundlsee, im Hintergrunde der Saarstein
The Salzkammergut. The Toplitzsee and Grundlsee. In the background, the Saarstein
Le Salzkammergut et les lacs : Toplitzsee et Grundlsee ; arrière-plan le Saarstein

Am Traunsee . . . zum Trocknen aufgehängte Fischernetze
The Traunsee . . . with fishermen's nets drying in the morning sunshine
Le Traunsee dans le Salzkammergut . . . le soleil et les filets séchant au
bord du lac créent un motif du plus bel effet

...aunsee mit Blick auf das Seeschloß Orth
...aunsee looking towards Schloss Orth
...e Traunsee avec vue sur le château d'Orth

67

Der weltberühmte Kurort Badgastein
The world-famous spa Badgastein
Badgastein, station thermale de tout temps réputée dans le monde

Alm mit Blick gegen Bischofsmü
Alpine pasture with Bischofsmü
Alpage au pied de la Bischofsmü

71

Der Mirabellgarten in Salzburg
Salzburg. The Mirabell-Garden
Le Jardin-Mirabel, Salzbourg

Der Residenzbrunnen vor dem Dom in Salzb
The Residenzbrunnen in front of the Cathedral, Salzb
Bassin de la fontaine de la Résidence devant la cathédrale, Salzbo

72

Wasserspiele im Lustschloß Hellbrunn
Hellbrunn Palace near Salzburg. The fountains
La château de plaisance de Hellbrunn. Ses fontaines

75

...ernhaus, im Hintergrund der Hochkönig
...mhouse with the Hochkönig in the background
...me, à l'arrière-plan le Hochkönig

Die Krimmler Wasserfälle
The waterfalls at Krimml, Salzburg
Les cascades de Krimml

77

Bergsteiger auf dem Gipfel des Kleinglockners
Mountaineers on the summit of the Kleinglockner
Alpinistes au sommet du Kleinglockner

Die Talsperren des Großkraftwerkes Kaprun in den Hohen Tau
The dams of the hydro-electric power station at Kaprun in the Tauern mounta
Ce barrage fait partie des installations hydroélectriques de Kaprun dans les Hohen Tau

nnensee im Stubaital, Tirol
ubaital, Tyrol. The Rinnensee
Rinnensee, lac alpestre du Stubaital, Tyrol

Eiskaskaden in der Rieseneishöhle des Dachsteins
Ice cascades in the mammoth Dachstein Caves
Cascades de glace dans les Grottes Géantes du Dachstein

am Hange des Kaisergebirges, Tirol
ine pasture with Kaisergebirge, Tyrol
age dans le massif du Kaisergebirge, Tyrol

Die Festung der Grenzstadt Kufstein, Tirol
The castle at Kufstein, Tyrol
La ville frontalière de Kufstein, et sa forteresse, Tyrol

83

Die Gletscherwelt im Ötztal, Tirol
Glaciers in the Ötztal, Tyrol
Les glaciers de l'Oetztal, Tyrol

Kitzbühel, Tirol
Kitzbühel, Tyrol
Kitzbühel, Tyrol

uben am Arlberg
uben at the foot of the Arlberg Pass
uben au pied de l'Arlberg

Holzarbeiter im Winter. Tirol
Woodmen in winter. Tyrol
Bûcherons en hiver. Tyrol

Das Goldene Dachl in der Altstadt von Innsbruck
The Goldene Dachl (gilded roof) in the old quarter of Innsbruck
Le Goldene Dachl (Petit Toit d'Or), dans le vieux quartier d'Innsbruck

Die Maria-Theresien-Straße in Innsbru
The Maria Theresien Strasse in Innsbru
La Maria Theresien Strasse de Innsbru

Der Ahornboden im Karwendel, Tirol
The Ahornboden in the Karwendel-range
Les montagnes du Karwendel. Ahornboden

Zillertaler Schütz
Marksmen of Ziller
Milicien paysan de la vallée de Zi

Penken im Zillertal, Tirol
Penken in the Zillertal, Tyrol
Penken dans le Zillertal, Tyrol

Der Fernpaß in T...
The Fernpass in Ty...
Le Fernpass, un col au Ty...

Kirche von Leiblfing in Tirol
e spire of the little church at Leiblfing, Tyrol
flèche élancée du clocher de l'église de Leiblfing, Tyrol

Almauftrieb im Karwendel
Cattle being driven to the Alpine pasture in the Karwendel
La transhumance dans le massif du Karwendel

Kühe auf der Alm im Karwendel, Tirol
Cattle on the Alpine pasture in the Karwendel, Tyrol
Bovins sur un alpage du Karwendel, Tyrol

Innerberg vor der Felskulisse des Rätikons, Vorarl
The village of Innerberg perches opposite the rocks of the Rätikon, Vorar
Innerberg à l'arrière plan l'imposante muraille rocheuse du Raetikon, Vorar

Lech, Vorarlberg ...

Seefeld, Tyr
internationale Zentren des Winterspo
international centres for wintersp
centres internationales des sports de ne

Skifahrer im Pulverschnee am Flexensattel
Ski-runners in powder snow on the Flexensattel
Virages dans la neige poudreuse du Flexensattel

"Nenzinger Himmel", Vorarlbe

Feldkirch. Die Schattenburg, Vorarlbergs bedeutendste Burg
Feldkirch. The Schattenburg, Vorarlberg's most important castle
Feldkirch. La Schattenburg, le plus important château-fort du Vorarlberg

Bregenz am Bodens
Bregenz on Lake Consta
Brégenz au bord du Lac de Constar

Valluga mit Pazieliernspitze und Schesaplana, Vorarlbe

Großglockner. Der Parkplatz beim Franz-Josephs-Haus, ein Treffpunkt der Welt
Grossglockner. Parking place at the Franz Josephs Haus, an international meeting-point
Grossglockner. Parc à voitures de la Franz Josephs Haus

Velden am Wörther
Velden on the Wörther
La plage de Velden, Wörther

dstock im Mölltal, Kärnten
wayside shrine in the Mölltal, Carinthia
age votive dans le Mölltal

Maria Wörth am Wörther See
Maria Wörth on the Wörther See
Maria Wörth, Wörther See

111

Badeszene am Wörther See
Bathing beach on the Wörther See
Sur une plage du Wörther See

Das Landhaus in Klagenf
Klagenfurt: The Landh
Le Landhaus, Klagenf

Maria Saal, Kärnten. Carinthia. Carinthie

Burg Hochosterwitz, das Wahrzeichen Kärnte
Burg Hochosterwitz, Carinthias best-known landm
Le château de Hochosterwitz, symbole de la Carint

Riedersburg, Steiermark. Styria. Styrie

Graz, die Hauptstadt Steiermark
A landmark in Graz, the capital of Styr
Graz, capitale de la Styr

Doppelwendeltreppe der Burg in Graz
Double-spiral Stairway of the Burg at Graz
Escalier tournant double au château de Graz

In der Bibliothek des Stiftes Admont, Steiermark
The library at the monastery of Admont, Sty.
La bibliothèque du monastère d'Admont, Sty.

Paddler auf der Salza, Steiermark
Paddling on the Salza, Styria
Canoëistes sur la Salza, Styrie

Segelboote auf dem Neusiedler See, Burgenl
Sailing boats on the Neusiedler See, Burgenl
Voiliers sur le Neusiedler See, Burgenl

120

Schilfernte im Burgenla
Reedworkers in Burgenla
La recolte du jo

Feste Forchtenstein, die bedeutendste Burg des Burgenlandes
...tenstein Castle, Burgenland
...rteresse de Forchtenstein, Burgenland

Bergkirche in Eisenstadt
The Bergkirche at Eisenstadt
Eglise à Eisenstadt

Der Schweinehirt in der Pußta des Burgenlandes
Swineherd in the Burgenland. Puszta
Gardien de troupeaux dans la Puszta du Burgenland

Zahlreiche Ziehbrunnen sieht man im viehreichen Burgen
The dairy farming province of Burgenland has a large number of these characteristic w
Les nombreux puits à chaîne du Burgenland, un pays riche en b

Abendstimmung auf dem Neusiedler See
Evening on the calm Neusiedler See
Crépuscule sur les bords du Neusiedler See